Survival First Aid Guide

How to Prepare for an
Emergency Situation

Table of Contents

INTRODUCTION

Some disasters are simply not survivable. But most are, and research on human behavior suggests that the difference between life and death often comes down to the simple – yet surprisingly difficult – task of recognizing threats before they overwhelm you, preparing adequately for them and then working through them as discrete challenges. The people who survive disasters and emergencies tend to be those who prepared for it, and they are more capable of making smart decisions under pressure because of their prior preparation. The ability to prepare for emergency is not a trait that some people are born with; almost anyone can learn them. Here's how to prepare yourself for an emergency situation.

It was early, 9:00AM, and eerily dark in Poway, Calif., as 75-mph winds drove chaparral embers through the air and shook the bones of Frank Vaplon's house. One ember lodged in his woodpile and set it ablaze. Geared up in a mail-order firefighter's outfit — helmet, bunker coat, respirator, the whole thing — Vaplon began his assault by shooting a high-pressure stream of water at the flames, but it just blew back against him in a hot mist. "It was like pissing into the wind," Vaplon says. "So I turned around and started spraying down the house."

The Witch Creek fire was the fourth largest on record in California. "The last thing I want from my story is for people to risk their lives," Vaplon says. "But I'd thought about protecting my home." The day before the fire swept through his 2.5-acre spread, he woke up early to the distant smell of smoke. He immediately broke out 500 feet of fire hose and attached it to a standpipe hooked up to a 10,000-gallon water tank. "I started watering down everything that I could," Vaplon says. "The roof, my lawn, everything."

The former Hewlett-Packard engineer didn't stop there. He raked up all the loose debris around his house, and then boarded up the attic vents where embers might get in. He checked the fuel for his three backup generators. And he put important papers in a steel box, which he loaded into his RV. He parked the vehicle facing out just in case he needed to bolt. "I had a plan to go if I had to go," he says. "If for one minute I started to get scared, I would have left."

The gear and setup were just part of Vaplon's extensive preparation. Whether deliberately or not, he had organized his brain to deal with disaster by planning a detailed fire strategy. He had done so much advance work that he had created a model for his brain to act on when disaster came. All his equipment would have been useless if he hadn't thought through how to use it. The Witch Creek blaze swept past in less than 2 minutes. Vaplon quickly put out the small fires on his property, then doused his neighbors' fires.

What is an Emergency?

An emergency is a situation that poses an immediate risk to health, life, property, or environment. Most emergencies require urgent intervention to prevent worsening of the situation, although in some situations, mitigation may not be possible and agencies may only be able to offer palliative care for the aftermath.

An incident, to be an emergency, conforms to one or more of the following, if it:

- Poses an immediate threat to life , health , property, or environment
- Has already caused loss of life, health detriments, property damage, or environmental damage
- Has a high probability of escalating to cause immediate danger to life, health, property, or environment.

Types of emergency

Dangers to life

Many emergencies cause an immediate danger to the life of people involved. This can range from emergencies affecting a single person, to incidents that affect large numbers of people such as natural disasters including tornadoes, hurricanes, floods, mudslides, fire outbreaks etc.

Dangers to health

Some emergencies are not necessarily immediately threatening to life, but might have serious implications for the continued health and well-being of a person or persons. The causes of a 'health' emergency are often very similar to the causes of an emergency threatening to life, which includes emergencies of natural disasters etc.

Dangers to the environment

Some emergencies do not immediately endanger life, health or property, but do affect the natural environment and creatures living within it. Examples would include forest fires and marine oil spills.

Types of disasters:

- Natural and
- Man-made

A natural disaster can happen at any time. Some disasters give warning like a storm preceding a flood. Others, like earthquakes or tsunamis, give no warning. Once a disaster happens, the time to prepare is gone and all you can do is cope. Take the next few minutes to examine what you can do to prepare. Anything you do today will be like making a deposit in your survivability savings account for withdrawal in tough times. Examples of natural disasters are:

- Earthquakes
- Extreme Heat
- Floods
- Hurricanes
- Landslides
- Tornadoes
- Tsunamis
- Volcanoes

- Wildfires
- Winter
- Severe Weather
- Flu Pandemics

Examples of man-made disasters are:

- Blackouts (where large areas lose power)
- Terrorist Attacks
- Oil Spills
- Accidental Forest Fire

You could be just about anywhere when a disaster strikes: in the bathroom, driving to the store, sitting at your desk at work, or in the back yard. But remember, you will most likely be caught unaware unless you are prepared.

Since life can change in an instant, it makes sense to be prepared. "The best thing you can do is be ready for an emergency," says Mary Margaret Walker, a spokesperson for the U.S. Federal Emergency Management Agency (FEMA).

CHAPTER 1

PREPARING THE HOME, WORK AND SCHOOL

How can I prepare for an emergency, like a natural or man-made disaster? This is a very important question that every soul who has gotten to the age of accountability should not only ask himself/herself but also proffer the needed answer to. The question now is not whether or not emergency situations will come but that of how to handle them when they do.

How to Prepare

Learn about the types of natural disasters that are most likely to occur in your area (hurricanes, floods, etc.) and how best to prepare for each. Consider taking an emergency preparation class. Local governments, healthcare centers, and the American Red Cross offer courses on first aid, cardiopulmonary resuscitation (CPR), and disaster response that can help you prepare for an emergency close to home.

With luck, you'll never have to use what you learn, but it may give you peace of mind to know that you're ready for a natural disaster or other emergency.

Rather than shield your child or family members, it's best to educate and involve everyone in emergency preparations. Teach your child what to do. Teach your child when and how to call emergency response center or 911, and where to meet outside the house if there's a fire or another reason to evacuate quickly. Your child can also help you assemble an emergency supply kit. It's a good idea to review emergency procedures with your child a couple of times in a year too.

Develop an emergency plan. Figure out how your family can get out of the house quickly, and practice this escape route regularly. Also, designate a nearby meeting place – the tree across the street or the corner mailbox, for example – if a fire, flood, earthquake, or other event forces you out of your home.

Plan for a few contingencies based on your usual schedule (what to do if you're at work and your child is at daycare, for instance). The last thing you want is to have to search for each other in the chaos, or find out your child stayed inside during a fire because he didn't know where to go.

Create a list of emergency numbers. When you're in the middle of a crisis, it's not always easy to find or remember important phone numbers. So program your phone with emergency numbers, including work, school, and daycare. Also include contact information of neighbors, family doctors, ambulance services, nearby hospitals, the gas Company, and local police, fire, and health departments.

Make sure your partner and your child's caregivers have copies of your email address because email might work when phones don't. You might even want to program the lock screen on your phone with your emergency contact information in case someone needs to help you.

Choose an out-of-area emergency contact person. During a disaster, local phone lines and cell towers may go down or become so overloaded with calls that it's difficult to get in touch with anyone in your area. That's why you might want to consider choosing an out-of-area relative or friend to be your family's backup contact person.

Be sure that you and your child's caregivers have that person's personal phone, work phone, and email address with you so that you can exchange messages about how you're doing, where you are, and other vital information.

Some Things You Can Do to Prepare

In each section below we have provided a list of "things to do" to prepare, as well as a list of recommended supplies. The largest list is for items slanted mostly for your home. After all, home is where you have the largest space available for your supplies. This is an ideal list and we realize that some of these items might be a bit out of reach for many. We recommend starting small and slowly building up your supplies over time as your finances permit. Look the list over, and try to understand why some of the items are listed. What we all really need to survive is food, water, and shelter. Beyond these three categories, everything else is just for comfort. But again, anything you can put away now may be greatly appreciated if you are ever in time of need!

Be prepared at Home

Install and regularly check smoke detectors. Know how to shut off your water, gas, and electric service if local officials instruct you to. If you shut off the gas, only a qualified professional should turn it back on. And if you don't know where your shut-offs are, ask your utility company.

You need to have supplies on hand at each location. It may sound like overkill, but you can't expect all three locations to be unscathed if a large disaster strikes. If you store provisions at each location, you will cover most of the likely situations. Another note: pets may not be allowed into shelters for health and space reasons. Prepare an emergency pen for pets in the home that includes, at a minimum, a three (3) day supply of dry food and a large container of water.

Home is where you can do the most to be prepared. But remember that you are only home for about 1/2 of the hours in a day. You must also be prepared at work, and have additional supplies in your car.

Strap gas appliances to walls or floor, especially the water heater. Remember your water heater is a large source of water, and weighs several hundred pounds when full. A four hundred pound water heater will break gas lines on its way to the floor. Gas appliances are a real danger in an earthquake, and are the cause of most fires after a quake. Verify your house is bolted to its foundation.

Repair defective electrical wiring and leaky gas connections. These are potential fire risks. Brace overhead light fixtures. Replace solid gas lines with flexible lines on stoves, water heaters, and dryers. Nail plywood on top of ceiling joists inside the attic to protect people from chimney bricks that could fall through the ceiling.

Find out where the utility shut-offs are for water, power, and gas. Place a flashlight or an emergency light next to your breaker panel. Place a wrench in your water meter box located near the street. Place or attach a "4-in-1 Tool" on your gas meter for turning off the gas. Evaluate each room in your house. Ask yourself: what will fall on my head, or will keep me from getting out if it fell? Secure anything you find. Hang heavy items such as pictures and mirrors away from beds, couches, and anywhere people sit. Fasten shelves securely to walls and place large or heavy objects on lower shelves. Store breakable items such as bottled foods, glass, and china in low, closed cabinets with latches. Store household chemicals on a bottom shelf of a closed cabinet. Never store bleach and ammonia in the same cabinet. These chemicals, when mixed, will create a toxic gas as deadly as any ever created.

Identify the best and worst places to be in your house. Remember that you might not have any choice as to where you will be located when a disaster strikes. The best places inside the house are under major beams that are secured to the rest of the structure, or in strong doorways, or inner structural walls. The worst places are in front of windows, or near fireplaces and chimneys.

Make an emergency plan including escape routes and meeting places. Choose both a nearby meeting place and an out-of-state relative to be your check-in contact for the family.

Plug emergency lighting into selected outlets. These flashlights are constantly charged, and turn on automatically when power fails, or when the units are unplugged.

Keep all tree and shrub limbs trimmed so they don't come in contact with wires.

Keep trees adjacent to buildings free of dead or dying wood.

Store combustible or flammable materials in approved safety containers and keep them away from the house.

Be Prepared at Work

Read your company's evacuation plan! Note the designated meeting locations for after an evacuation. Each time you enter a room, take note of the exit routes and locations of fire extinguisher and medical kits. Note locations of stairways as you walk from location to location.

Keep your own personal supplies in your desk in a single pack of some kind that you can access quickly. Along with your supplies, store a pair of walking shoes.

Be sure you have composed a card to carry in your wallet or purse with important phone numbers including the number of your out-of-state phone contact. Keep the area under your desk free of waste-paper baskets and the like. This 6 square foot area might be home during a few traumatic moments.

If you are not at your desk when something happens, don't count on being able to make it back. Store additional supplies in your car.

Take a look around your work site. You will find that state and federal regulations have required your employer to have fire extinguishers and first aid kits at key locations. Some employers are beginning to place chemical light sticks and other emergency supplies in some areas as well, but you should probably plan for the worst. You need the supplies to be on your own for a minimum of three days. It may take you that long to get home, and don't count on your car being accessible especially if you park in a building parking structure.

Be Prepared at School

Contact your local school district to obtain policy regarding how children will be released from school. Know the location of the nearest police and fire stations, as well as the route to the nearest hospital emergency room.

Meet with neighbors and find out who has medical experience.

If you are taking this preparedness thing seriously, share this information with the households next to you. The more people you can convince to prepare, the greater your group resources. Remember that you will be called upon by all around you for help, especially by those who didn't take warnings seriously. (Remember Noah?)

Give spare keys to your trusted neighbors. Show them where the utility shut-offs are and provide them with a list of contact phone numbers. Ask how to turn off your neighbor's utilities.

What about the emergency plan at my child's daycare, school, or camp?

Be familiar with the emergency plan at your child's daycare, school, or camp.

If you can't get to daycare, school, or camp right away during an emergency, for instance, the caregiver will need to know who will pick up your child – such as a designated grandparent or a neighbor – and how to contact them. If the building has to be evacuated because of a fire, chemical contamination, or other problems, you'll need to know where your children will be taken and how long they'll be kept there.

CHAPTER 2

PREPARATION FOR WATER

Whenever some crisis happens, there is no time left for preparation. However, if you are prepared to meet crisis before time, you will feel more comfortable to meet the emergency situations. Being prepared for emergencies or disasters is extremely important in this ever changing world. It is even more crucial for disabled persons or people with special needs. The ability to successfully meet emergency situations is mainly dependent on preparedness before occurrence of any disaster. Though being prepared doesn't entirely mean survivability, but it greatly enhances chances of your survival from any kind of tragedy. However, you need to have essential items with you to cope with disaster situations. One of the very important items is food.

Water is the most essential ingredient to survive for a human being. Humans need water not just for preparing food but also for cooking and staying hygienic. A person requires 1 gallon of water per day to survive and one need to be prepared enough to arrange for water in crisis situations. Every person must have a reserve for at least 3 days for evacuation and a 2-week supply at home. It is of no doubt that a human can live many days without food, but not without water. Even a thirst for few hours can make someone feel terrible.

30 gallons per person (2 gallons per person per day for 1 week). This might sound excessive, but look at your water bill this month! This figure assumes that when at home, you will occasionally want a sponge bath, or cook something like pasta or rice. You might even wash your hair or clothes, and will eventually flush a toilet. Large food grade 55 gallon plastic drums are ideal for bulk water storage. A good location is in your detached garage. Remember that your water heater in the

house is typically 50 gallons, and may be used if your dwelling survives.

Additional water may be purchased in single-use plastic bottles, and should be stored away from the house or garage. Remember that these water bottles will need to be rotated out since they have a limited shelf life unless water treatment is used. Keep at least a three-day supply of bottled water for each family member. Allow for 1 gallon per person per day (2 quarts for drinking and 2 quarts for sanitation).

Nursing mothers, children, and the elderly or sick need slightly more, and you may need to include more water in hot weather or for disinfecting. You'll also need more if you have pets.

Store the above items in large, unused, covered garbage cans or in duffel bags. Because many emergencies tend to disrupt power, food, and water supplies, these items will serve you well in most circumstances (See FEMA's complete list of emergency supplies)

CHAPTER 3

PREPARATION FOR FOOD

Everybody knows the importance of food in his life. It is of great importance to have a stock of food for at least 2 weeks to meet some crisis. However, a person can survive for more than one week without food, though nobody wants to stay hungry. It is recommended that we bring some extra stock of food items every time we go for shopping. However, it is also essential to check for their expiry dates and try to bring items that can last for longer periods. Make sure to replace it in and out to preserve freshness.

Canned goods – ready to eat soups, meats, veggies and fruit. The same type of food you normally have on hand. Make a point to start buying extra of whatever you normally buy, to dedicate to your supplies. Date the top of anything you buy with a black permanent marker.

Plan for a minimum of three (3) cans per person per day for a week (about two mixed cases per person). Store these items in suitcases near corners of the house. Additional food should be stored in the garage, and at another location away from the dwelling. Pay close attention to how the packaging will hold up to damp environments. Cans will rust unless you protect them. A good way to protect an item for damp storage is to put it in a zip lock bag, then pack it inside a food grade plastic bucket (with lid). Remember to maximize canned goods with moisture content like ready to eat soup. Don't forget a manual can opener! No power, no way to open cans!

MREs - meals ready to eat. These are ideal for outside storage. Remember, the key is to distribute your supplies at various locations. These may be stored in the worst of conditions.

Long shelf life with no rotation. Long shelf life Freeze-dried or Dehydrated foods. But remember, these items require water.

Non-perishable food and eating supplies. Pack a manual (not electric) can opener, paper cups, plates, and utensils. Pack a three-day supply of food for each family member, including items like powdered milk or formula and canned fruit, meat, soup, vegetables, and juice.

Don't forget food for babies or those with special dietary needs. Baby formula can get damaged by heat or cold, so protect it from temperature extremes. Check expiration dates every six months and replace items accordingly.

Supplies

- Cooking
- Barbecue grill
- 40 pounds charcoal
- 2 cans of starter fluid

Or a propane unit with two 20-pound containers of propane. A propane camp stove may also be used.

- Pot(s) and pan(s) for cooking
- Kitchen knife
- Silverware: spoon, fork
- Styrofoam cups
- Waterproof matches or lighter
- Zip lock bags
- Can Opener!
- Aluminum foil. A must! Can be formed into just about anything you might need.

CHAPTER 4

PREPARATION FOR SHELTER

Shelter is a basic necessity of life. Especially, in disaster conditions, everyone needs a safe location. The ideal condition however is to stay at home. But if someone thinks that his home is not a safe place, then he might need to find some relative who can provide him shelter in emergency condition. Also, if anybody doesn't have any relative where he can stay, government or Red Cross usually provides places for shelter. However, in any case, everyone needs to be prepared enough to meet such circumstances. Being prepared to survive in any disaster is best not for you but also for your family.

Two person tube tent minimum (larger size better)

Wool blanket or sleeping bag

Emergency space blanket

Instant hand/body warming pads

Propane-powered heater, 20-pound cylinder mounted

CHAPTER 5

EMERGENCY MATERIALS

Along with the food, water and shelter, everybody needs to have some essential items like first aid kit and medicine for at least more than a week. Along with medical equipment, you also need to have some sanitation tools, a camping stove, warm clothing, LED lights and lanterns with extra batteries. Lastly, one must have some kind of self-defense. Anyone can simply figure out what he need with a little online surfing and see what he needs for such circumstances. For self-defense, you need to buy weapons like handgun or rifle with ammunition. Also, do some practice on regular basis to get at least some basic skills.

Life is priceless; provisions saves life. Always be prepared with survival skills to cope with all situations that can happen in your life. Also, it is recommended to keep it simple and go for necessities only. Educate your family and yourself for probable incidents and disasters that can occur in the community. Realize the importance of being prepared in advance, make a plan and start working on it.

- Medicine and first aid supplies. Key items include sterile adhesive bandages and pads, antiseptic lotion, a thermometer, tweezers, scissors, latex gloves, and an over-the-counter pain reliever. In addition, ask your doctor or pharmacist about getting a second set of crucial prescription medications to store in your disaster kit – bearing in mind that they can be damaged by heat and cold. Don't pack them unless you plan to store your kit in a temperate location. If you do decide to stock crucial medications, check the expiration dates every few months and replace as needed.

- An extra set of car keys.

- A hand-cranked or battery-powered radio. You'll want to tune in for regular updates on the situation and evacuation instructions.

- A flashlight. Power outages are almost certain, no matter the nature of the disaster.

- Extra batteries.

- Cash or traveler's checks. Don't count on being able to access an ATM. A credit card should do for expenses like gas, food, and lodging, but it won't work if the power is out. It never hurts to have some money tucked away for unexpected expenses.

- Important documents. At some point you'll need access to important documents like wills, deeds, passports, birth and marriage certificates, and insurance papers, especially if you have to abandon your house or leave the area.

- You may not want to keep these in an emergency kit, but it might be helpful to have copies. (Store the real documents in a waterproof, fireproof container.)

- Sanitation supplies. Keep a stash of toilet paper, soap, toothbrushes, toothpaste, deodorant, tampons, sanitary pads, diapers, and wipes in your kit.

- Clothes and bedding. Pack a change of clothes and a sturdy pair of shoes for each family member, along with a sleeping bag.

- Games and books. If the power goes out, you won't have a computer or other device to help pass the time. A stash of books, games, and toys will help keep everyone in good spirits.

CHAPTER 6

CONCLUSION

Planning ahead can help keep you and your family safe if there's an emergency, like a natural or man-made disaster.

Emergencies can happen at any time, so it's important to make sure you and your family are ready. Here's what you can do:

- Get an emergency supply kit.
- Make a family emergency plan.
- Learn what to do in different types of emergencies.
- Take Action!

Find out how to keep cold food safe when there's a power outage.
Put all of your important documents in one place so they are easy to find in an emergency.

Use these activity books to involve your kids in preparing for an emergency.

Take Action!

Make an emergency supply kit

Gather supplies like water, medicines, and blankets. You won't have time to search or shop for these supplies during an emergency, so put your kit together now. Make sure your kit includes:

- Water for at least 3 days. You'll need at least 1 gallon of water a day for each person. Don't forget water for your pets, too!
- Food for at least 3 days. Choose foods that don't need to be kept cold and that you don't need to cook, like energy bars, peanut butter, crackers, and canned fruit. Don't forget a can opener!
- Prescription medicine that you take every day, like heart or diabetes medicine.

- A first aid kit to treat cuts, burns, and other basic injuries. Find out what to put in your family's first aid kit. (You can also buy first aid kits at many stores.)
- A battery-powered radio with extra batteries or a hand crank radio.
- A flashlight and extra batteries.
- A whistle to call for help.

Some people may need extra help in an emergency:

- Older adults.
- People with disabilities.
- People with pets.

Keep your emergency supplies together in a backpack, bag, or easy-to-carry container. Use a waterproof container if possible. Store your supplies in a place that's easy to reach.

Make a plan

It's important to make a plan in case your family members aren't in the same place when disaster strikes. Be sure to decide on an emergency contact – a person that each member of your family knows to call during an emergency.

Sit down and fill it out together so that everyone in your family knows what to do. Ask everyone to keep a copy in their wallet, purse, or backpack.

Find out about plans at school and work.
Places where you and your family spend the most time, like school and work, may have their own emergency plans. Ask your employer and your child's school for a copy of their emergency plan. Ask school or work about their emergency plan.

Know what to do during different types of emergencies

Contact your state's emergency management office to find out what types of disasters are most common in your area. Ask if your community has an emergency response plan.

Plan ahead for how you could take action in different types of situations. For example:

Evacuate means leaving the area. Think about friends or relatives you could stay with in another town. What could you do with your pets? Get tips on how to plan for an evacuation.

Shelter in place means taking shelter wherever you are – like at home, work, school, or in your car. In some emergencies, this is safer than leaving. Find out how to shelter in place.

Quarantine and isolation means keeping sick people (or people who might be sick) away from other people to keep diseases from spreading. Find out more about quarantine and isolation. Always listen to local warnings to help you decide what to do.

Water Containers (Cleaning and Storage)

Unopened commercially bottled water is the safest and most reliable emergency water supply.

Use of food-grade water storage containers, such as those found at surplus or camping supply stores, is recommended if you prepare stored water yourself. Before filling them with safe water, use these steps to clean and sanitize storage containers:

1. Wash the storage container with dishwashing soap and water and rinse completely with clean water.

2. Sanitize the container by adding a solution made by mixing 1 teaspoon of unscented

liquid household chlorine bleach in one quart of water.

3. Cover the container and shake it well so that the sanitizing bleach solution touches all inside surfaces of the container.

4. Wait at least 30 seconds and then pour the sanitizing solution out of the container.

5. Let the empty sanitized container air-dry before use OR rinse the empty container with clean, safe water that already is available.

Avoid using the following containers to store safe water:

- Containers that cannot be sealed tightly
- Containers that can break, such as glass bottles
- Containers that have ever been used for any toxic solid or liquid chemicals (includes old bleach containers)
- Plastic or cardboard bottles, jugs, and containers used for milk or fruit juices

For proper water storage,

- Label container as "drinking water" and include storage date.
- Replace stored water that is not commercially bottled every six months.
- Keep stored water in a place with a fairly constant cool temperature.
- Do not store water containers in direct sunlight.
- Do not store water containers in areas where toxic substances such as gasoline or pesticides are present.
- During an emergency, learn how to Make Water Safe and about Finding Emergency Water Sources.

Note: Caffeinated drinks and alcohol dehydrate the body, which increases the need for drinking water.

Lastly, even if anyone is facing emergency only for a 48 or 72 hours, he will need to have some books, playing cards, and board games available to help you kill time. Remember, we can face emergency for longer periods and there is nothing to do in such situations. So, it is very much crucial to have such things that can help us kill time. It might even contain some candies as well as crayons and coloring books for kids. Also, check for extra mobile batteries. However, it could take some extra effort and time to stock up such things, but in the end this will be helpful for your survival.

www.ingramcontent.com/pod-product-compliance
Lightning Source LLC
Chambersburg PA
CBHW071146280526
45787CB00003B/1426